CSI

Analyzing Data

Andrew Einspruch

Publishing Credits

Editor
Sara Johnson

Editorial Director
Dona Herweck Rice

Editor-in-Chief
Sharon Coan, M.S.Ed.

Creative Director
Lee Aucoin

Publisher
Rachelle Cracchiolo, M.S.Ed.

Image Credits

The author and publisher would like to gratefully credit or acknowledge the following for permission to reproduce copyright material: cover Photodisc; p.1 Photodisc; p.4 The Photolibrary; p.5 Alamy/Pablo Paul; p.6 Alamy/UpperCut Images; p.8 Shutterstock; p.9 The Photolibrary; p.10 Shutterstock; p.12 Shutterstock; p.14 Shutterstock; p.16 Shutterstock; p.17 The Photolibrary; p.18 Shutterstock; p.20 Alamy/Pablo Paul; p.21 Shutterstock; p.22 Alamy/Pablo Paul; p. 24 The Photolibrary; p. 26 Alamy/Stock Connection Distribution; p.27 The Photolibrary; p.28 Corbis; Getty Images; Photo Disc

While every care has been taken to trace and acknowledge copyright, the publishers tender their apologies for any accidental infringement where copyright has proved untraceable. They would be pleased to come to a suitable arrangement with the rightful owner in each case.

Teacher Created Materials

5301 Oceanus Drive
Huntington Beach, CA 92649-1030
http://www.tcmpub.com
ISBN 978-0-7439-0921-1

Table of Contents

At the Crime Scene	4
What Investigators Need to Know	6
Fingerprints	8
Blood and Blood Types	12
Genetic Identification	16
Fibers and Fragments	20
Lie Detectors	24
Solving a Crime	27
Problem-Solving Activity	28
Glossary	30
Index	31
Answer Key	32

At the Crime Scene

A crime has been **committed**! No one knows how it happened or who committed the crime. The police arrive at the crime scene. They have no obvious clues and no reliable **witnesses**.

A car pulls up and a team of **forensic** (fuh-REN-sik) **investigators** gets out. They are here to figure out what happened. They put on special suits. They put covers over their shoes so they do not **contaminate** (kuhn-TAM-uh-nate) the crime scene. They collect data, or clues. These clues are sometimes so tiny that they cannot be seen without special equipment.

Forensic investigators collect **evidence** (EV-i-duhns) at the scene of a crime.

When a crime is committed, the police hunt for clues. They hope to find the **perpetrator** (PER-puh-tray-tur). They might find a weapon or car used to commit the crime. Each clue the police find helps to reduce the number of **suspects**.

Forensic investigators do the same thing, but with different types of clues. They hunt for fingerprints and blood. They search for hairs, **fibers**, and even dirt. They figure out the best way to collect such data. Then they conduct tests with the data and **analyze** the results.

An investigator photographs a shoe print at a crime scene.

Forensic Science

Forensic investigators design data investigations to gather evidence and answer questions about a crime. Later, the investigators may show their evidence in a court of law.

What Investigators Need to Know

Crime scene investigators (CSIs) need to know more than just "who did it." Investigators look at the 5 Ws. These are who, what, where, when, and why. They also look at H (how).

- **WHO:** This could include who the **victim** is, as well as who the perpetrator is.
- **WHAT:** This covers what happened.
- **WHERE:** This involves possible crime scenes, such as where the crime was committed. It also covers where a victim was found.
- **WHEN:** Knowing when a crime happened helps investigators. They can rule out suspects. Some suspects may have **alibis** (AL-uh-bys).
- **WHY:** Investigators need to know the reason why a crime happened.
- **HOW:** This covers how the perpetrator planned and carried out the crime.

CRIME SCENE DO NOT CROSS

Data about the time of day that car thefts took place has been collected. This helps investigators **predict** when these crimes are more likely to occur in the future. Use the data in the graph to answer the questions below.

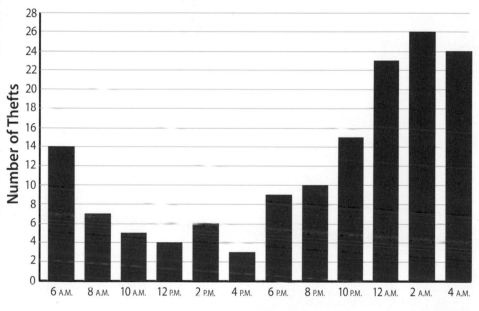

Crookville Car Thefts

a. At what time did the fewest number of car thefts occur?

b. How many car thefts occured at 8 A.M.?

c. At what times do you think the most patrol cars should be sent out? Use the data to explain your answer.

Fingerprints

Did you know that no two people's fingerprints are the same? Even identical twins have different fingerprints. Your fingerprints formed before you were even born. They stay the same for your entire life.

Thousands of years ago, fingerprints were used to identify people in Ancient Babylon. But it wasn't until 1892 that fingerprints were first used to prove someone committed a crime.

Why Do We Have Fingerprints?

We have tiny **ridges** on our fingers so that we can grip things. If we didn't have these ridges, objects would slip through our fingers easily! These ridges make our fingerprints.

The skin ridges on our fingers and thumbs form our fingerprints. These ridges leave a mark when we touch something. Forensic investigators can also use prints from palms, toes, feet, and ears.

A fingerprint found at a crime scene can be compared with fingerprints in a police **database**. It can also be compared with a fingerprint taken from a suspect. Forensic investigators work to match parts of 2 fingerprints that look the same.

A forensic scientist compares fingerprints. The yellow markers are used to point out the features being compared.

Fingerprint Patterns

Fingerprints tend to have 3 basic patterns: arch, loop, and whorl.

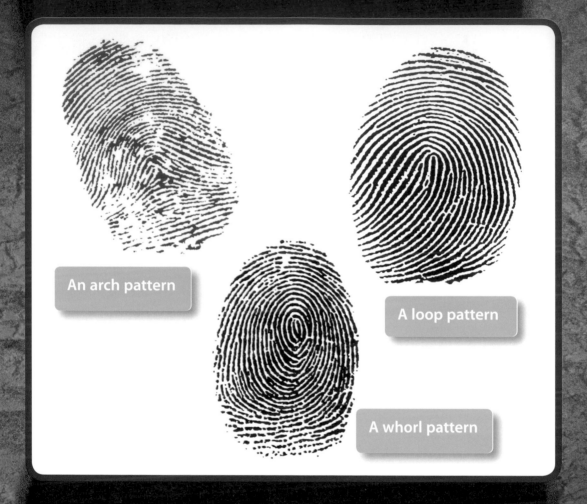

An arch pattern

A loop pattern

A whorl pattern

These basic patterns can be put into more **specific** groups. For example, 60% to 70% of people have fingerprints that are some kind of loop. These patterns have more specific names like plain loop and twinned loop.

Today, computer systems compare fingerprints. A whole, clear fingerprint may often result in a match. But sometimes a fingerprint found at a crime scene is not whole or clear. The system gives a list of possible matches. The investigators do more research.

LET'S EXPLORE MATH

A fingerprint was found at a crime scene. It came from the thumb of someone's right hand. The police looked at their fingerprint database. Use the data in the table to answer the questions below.

a. The CSIs know the perpetrator is over 45 years of age. How many suspects do they have in their database that match that description?

Ages and Fingerprint Types

Type of Fingerprint	Age Groups (Years)			
	18–25	26–35	36–44	45+
Loop	24	37	41	28
Whorl	13	18	14	15
Arch	1	0	3	1

b. Fingerprint tests came back from the lab. They showed that the perpetrator has a whorl print. How many suspects do the police have now?

c. Which age group in the police database contains the most people?

Blood and Blood Types

Blood found at a crime scene provides forensic investigators with lots of data. They can test to see if the blood is human or animal. They can find out if the blood belongs to more than one person. They can check to see if the blood belongs to the victim or the perpetrator.

If investigators find human blood, they can figure out its type. Human blood can be sorted into four main types: type A, type B, type AB, and type O.

A lab **technician** (tek-NISH-uhn) tests blood samples.

Investigators found some blood at a crime scene. The police database showed the blood types of known criminals living in the area. There were 400 criminals on the database. Use the data in the circle graph to answer the questions below.

Blood Types of Criminals

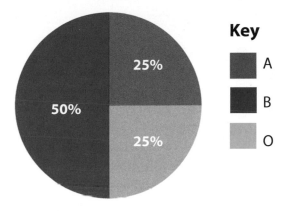

Key

- A
- B
- O

a. If the blood sample was type O, how many suspects would police have?

b. If the blood sample was type A or type B, how many suspects would they have for each blood type?

c. The results from the lab show that the blood type is AB. What might police **conclude** about the perpetrator, given the blood-type information?

Knowing blood types from the crime scene means the list of suspects gets smaller. In the United States, only 4% of people have type AB blood. So if the crime scene blood is type AB, then most suspects are ruled out. But if the crime scene blood is type O, it will not be very helpful to investigators. Type O is the most common blood type in the United States (45%).

Blood Types in the United States

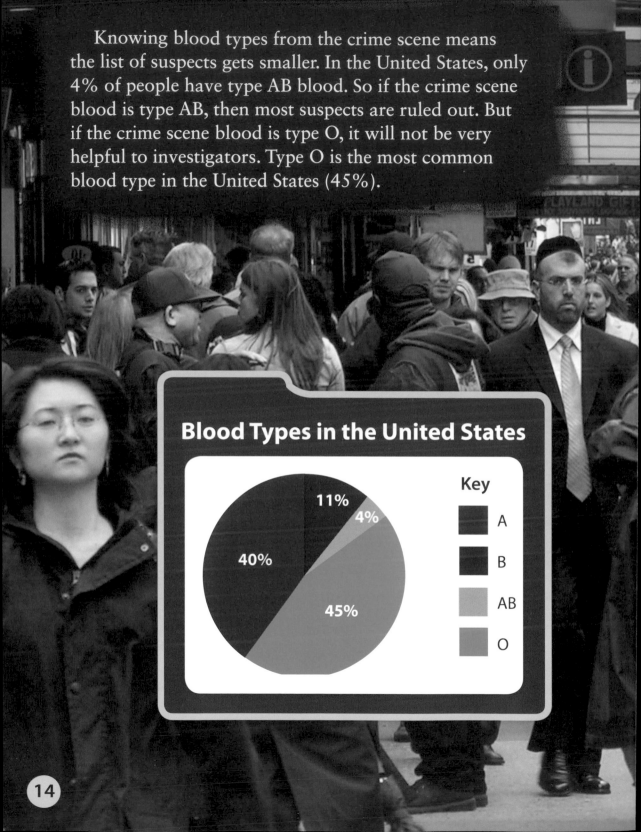

11%
4%
40%
45%

Key

A

B

AB

O

Blood types can include or **exclude** certain peoples or nationalities. For example, almost 100% of Native South Americans have blood type O. Blood types B and AB are very rare among Aboriginal Australians. The table below shows blood types of different peoples from around the world.

LET'S EXPLORE MATH

Blood Types of Different Peoples

Peoples	Blood Types			
	O	A	B	AB
British	46%	42%	9%	3%
Irish	52%	35%	10%	3%
French	43%	45%	9%	3%
Japanese	30%	38%	22%	10%
Aboriginal Australians	44%	56%	0%	0%

Use the data set in the table to answer these questions:

a. What percentage of British people have blood type B?

b. Which 3 peoples have a higher percentage of people with blood type A than type O?

c. Which blood type would you say is the rarest? Give reasons for your answer.

d. Over 420,000 New York residents have Irish ancestry. Approximately how many of them have type B blood?

Genetic Identification

Although no 2 fingerprints are the same, sometimes investigators do make an incorrect match. In courts of law today, the most reliable evidence is **genetic** (juh-NET-ik) **identification**. This is also known as genetic fingerprinting or **DNA** profiling.

A double helix strand of DNA

What Is DNA?

Your body is made up of between 10 and 100 billion living **cells**! DNA is found inside nearly every cell in your body. DNA contains the "instructions" for how your body looks, grows, and works. Things like your body size, shape, and eye color are controlled by your DNA.

Forensic investigators take a sample of a suspect's blood. They can also take a sample of hair, sweat, or saliva. The suspect's DNA is then analyzed from the sample. Then this DNA can be compared with samples found at a crime scene.

A scientist examining DNA fragments

Identical Twins
Everyone's DNA is different—except for identical twins. At least their fingerprints are different!

Most genetic information is the same for all humans. So investigators must focus on the part of a person's DNA that is **unique**. This small part is different from person to person.

The DNA for each of these children is unique.

Forensic investigators can use DNA profiling to tell one person from another. But they cannot use it to find out what a person looks like. They cannot use it to find out a person's age or race. But investigators can use a DNA profile with other forensic information, such as fingerprints and blood type. This helps them to form a better picture of a suspect.

Crookville police have data on the eye color of known car thieves. Use the data in the graph to answer the questions below.

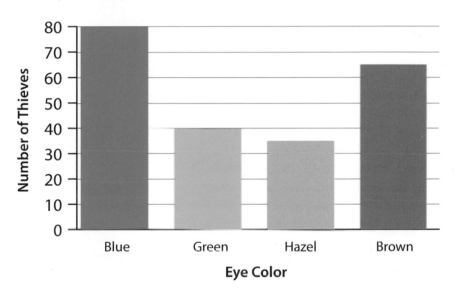

Eye Color of Crookville Car Thieves

a. How many of the car thieves have green eyes?

b. How many car thieves in total make up this data?

c. Which eye color has a data set of 65?

d. Which eye color would help an investigator focus on the fewest number of suspects?

Fibers and Fragments

Most people who commit a crime leave something behind. Or they take something away. It might be dirt, a hair, or a carpet fiber. These tiny items are called trace evidence. Forensic investigators look for trace evidence because it may link a suspect to a crime scene.

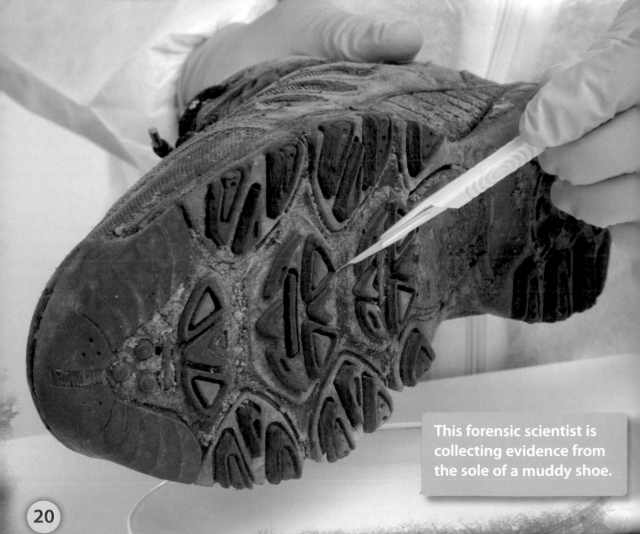

This forensic scientist is collecting evidence from the sole of a muddy shoe.

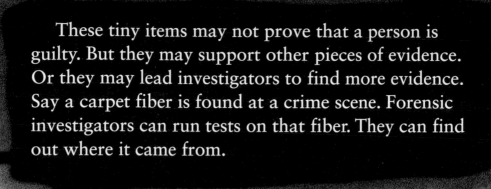

These tiny items may not prove that a person is guilty. But they may support other pieces of evidence. Or they may lead investigators to find more evidence. Say a carpet fiber is found at a crime scene. Forensic investigators can run tests on that fiber. They can find out where it came from.

Carpet fiber from a crime scene

Investigators analyze the fiber to find exactly what type of carpet it came from. They can see if the carpet is **synthetic** (sin-THET-ik) or natural. They can find out what dye was used. They can figure out what companies use that dye. They may be able to find out how much of the carpet was sold in a certain area. This helps them figure out how common the carpet is.

Unlike fingerprints, a carpet is probably not unique. There may have been miles of that type of carpet made. It may be in many houses all over the country. But that carpet may be in one suspect's house, and not in another's. Then, it is probable that the suspect with the matching carpet was at the crime scene.

At a crime scene, investigators found a red carpet fiber. Use the data in the table to answer the questions below.

Possible Suspects

Suspect	Carpet in House		Blood Type
	Color	Type	
Mr. A.	red	natural	O
Mr. X.	white	natural	O
Mr. Y.	red	natural	A
Ms. N.	red	synthetic	B
Ms. O.	white	natural	O
Mrs. P.	red	natural	A

a. Which suspects are eliminated based on the information above?

b. Results come back from the lab showing that the carpet fiber is natural. Which suspect can be eliminated now?

c. A sample of type A blood is found at the crime scene. Which suspect can be eliminated now?

d. Results come back from the lab showing that the DNA is female. Who is the most likely perpetrator of the crime?

Lie Detectors

All of this forensic evidence may lead police to a suspect. Investigators may then interview the suspect. They may use a polygraph (POL-i-graf). This is often known as a lie detector test.

A polygraph machine measures a person's blood pressure, heart rate, and breathing rate. These measurements are recorded on a moving piece of graph paper. Investigators believe these measurements show how nervous a person is. They believe that a person who is lying tends to be more nervous.

The graph paper printout from a polygraph machine

The interviewer starts with questions that have simple true or false answers. Then the interviewer asks about things that a person is likely to lie about. He or she may ask "Have you ever stolen something?" The lines on the graph paper can show if the person is telling the truth.

CSIs are interviewing a suspect about a robbery from a jewelry store. Look at this graph of the suspect's heart rate. This data was gathered using a polygraph. Use the data to answer the questions below. Remember, the higher a suspect's heart rate (beats per minute), the more likely it is that he or she is lying.

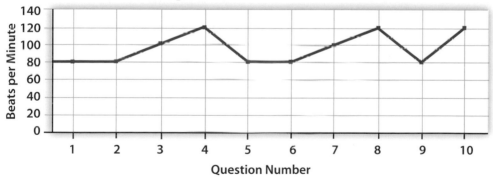

Suspect B's Heart Rate

a. Which questions do you think Suspect B answered truthfully?

b. Which questions do you think the suspect lied about?

c. Write a question that you think the suspect may have answered truthfully.

Polygraph results cannot always be used as evidence in court. Some people claim that they are almost completely accurate. Other people argue that the test itself makes a person nervous enough to fail. Studies have shown that polygraph tests are useful but, on the whole, not very accurate.

A polygraph test being taken in a police station

Solving a Crime

Forensic investigators need to find out how, when, where, and why a crime was committed, and by whom. They find clues and use these clues to figure out if a suspect is guilty.

Thanks to CSI data collection, there is no such thing as the perfect crime!

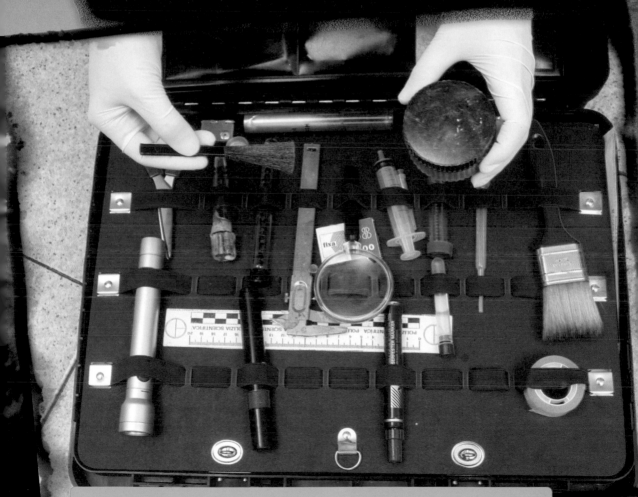

A CSI kit has the tools to find, collect, and record evidence at a crime scene. The brush and powder are used to find fingerprints.

Stolen Gems

In Robberville, precious gems have been stolen from a jewelry store. Crime scene investigators know that the criminal entered through a small window at the back of the store. The window is just over 7 feet above the ground. It is 24 inches wide and 24 inches high. They found a sample of type O blood. Yet, there was no ladder that the robber could have used to climb up to the window.

This table is the data file for possible suspects.

Suspects	Height	Weight (lb.)	Body Shape	Blood Type
Mr. J.	6 ft. 4 in.	240	large	O
Mr. S.	4 ft. 1in.	120	thin	O
Mrs. M.	5 ft. 3 in.	200	solid	A
Ms. D.	6 ft. 2 in.	135	thin	O
Mr. M.	6 ft. 2 in.	185	average	B
Ms. P.	4 ft. 4 in.	130	plump	O
Mrs. T.	5 ft. 1 in.	125	average	AB

Solve It!

a. Which suspect probably committed the crime?

b. Give reasons for your answer.

Use the steps below to help you find the data to justify your answers.

Step 1: A sample of blood type O was found at the crime scene. Make a list of the most likely suspects, based on this information.

Step 2: The window is just over 7 feet above the ground. Since there was no ladder, cross off the suspects who you believe could not have reached the window on their own. Explain your answer.

Step 3: The window was only 24 inches wide and 24 inches high. Look at the body shape and weight data of each suspect on your list. Cross off the suspect who you believe could not have fit through the window. Explain your answer.

Step 4: Look at your list of names. Which name is left? This name is your main suspect.

Glossary

analyze—examine in detail

alibis—the pleas made by suspects telling that they were at other places when crimes happened

cells—basic structural units of all life

committed—carried out

conclude—decide from available information

contaminate—to make something unclean. For a crime scene, this means adding things that might confuse investigators.

database—a computer program used for storing information

DNA—stands for deoxyribonucleic acid, which is the part of cells that carries genetic information

evidence—information that can help you decide if something is true or false

exclude—leave out

fibers—tiny threads

forensic investigators—people who look for evidence that will help police figure out who committed a crime

genetic identification—using DNA information to identify people

perpetrator—a person who committed a crime being investigate

predict—to guess what may happen in the future, based on observations and experiences

ridges—fine, raised lines on fingertip

specific—clearly defined or definite

suspects—people the police think may have committed a crime

synthetic—made artificially; not naturally made

technician—a person skilled in the details or techniques of a job

unique—the only one of its kind

victim—a person who has suffered as a result of a crime

witnesses—people who may have seen a crime taking place

Index

5 Ws, 6

alibis, 6

blood type(s), 12, 13, 14–15, 18, 23

carpet fiber, 21–22, 23

clues, 4, 5, 27

court (of law), 5, 16, 26

crime scene investigators (CSIs), 6, 11, 27

data, 4, 5, 7, 12, 19, 27

database, 9, 11, 13

dirt, 5, 20

DNA, 16–18, 23

DNA profiling, 16, 18

evidence, 4, 5, 16, 20, 21, 24, 26, 27

fiber(s), 5, 20–22

fingerprint patterns, 10–11

fingerprints, 5, 8–11, 16, 17, 18, 22, 27

forensic investigators, 4, 5, 9, 12, 17, 18, 20, 21, 27

genetic identification, 16–18

identical twins, 8, 17

perpetrator, 5, 6, 12, 23

police, 4, 5, 24, 26

polygraph (lie detector), 24–26

predict, 7

shoe print, 5

suspect, 5, 6, 9, 14, 18, 19, 20, 22, 23, 24

trace evidence, 20

victim, 6, 12

witnesses, 4

ANSWER KEY

Let's Explore Math

Page 7:
a. The fewest number of car thefts occured at 4 P.M.
b. 7 car thefts occurred at 8 A.M.
c. Hours will vary but should be between 10 P.M. and 6 A.M. Explanations will vary.

Page 11:
a. 44 suspects
b. 15 suspects
c. 36–44 age group

Page 13:
a. 25% of 400 criminals = 100 suspects for blood type O
b. 75% of 400 criminals = 300 suspects each for blood types A and B
c. Answers will vary but could include: the perpetrator is not in the database.

Page 15:
a. 9% of British people
b. French, Japanese, and Aboriginal Australians
c. Blood type AB is the rarest because it has the lowest percentage across all peoples in the data set.
d. 42,000 people

Page 19:
a. 40 car thieves
b. 220 car thieves
c. brown
d. hazel

Page 23:
a. Suspects Mr. X. and Ms. O. are eliminated.
b. Suspect Ms. N.
c. Suspect Mr. A.
d. Mrs. P.

Page 25:
a. Questions 1, 2, 5, 6, and 9
b. Questions 3, 4, 7, 8, and 10
c. Questions will vary.
Sample question: What is your name?

Problem-Solving Activity

a. Ms. D. probably committed the robbery.

b. Ms. D has blood type O. She is over 6 feet tall; she could reach the window without a ladder.
She has a thin body shape; she could easily have pulled herself through the small window.

Step 1: Mr. J., Mr. S., Ms. D., and Ms. P.

Step 2: Suspects Mr. S. and Ms. P. would be crossed off the list. They are both too short to reach up to the window and pull themselves through it.

Step 3: Suspect Mr. J. has a large body shape. He probably could not have fit through the small window.

Step 4: Suspect Ms. D. is left on the list.